brain bleeds silver linings

Bree Duwyn

Presentation by *BookLeaf Publishing*

Web: www.bookleafpub.com

E-mail: info@bookleafpub.com

ISBN: 9789357614214

First edition 2022

Dedicated to the order of the writers.

ACKNOWLEDGEMENT

I'd like to thank those who have supported my journey as a writer and who have helped me grow into who I am today.

To my parents who encouraged me to become anything I wanted and to always remind me how proud they are of what I have done and plan to do.

To my gramma, who is a constant light, always cheering me on.

To my brother, who had me complete so many assignments of his English homework, to say in the end of his studies that what I do is "art".

To my friends, both new and old, that have brought me joy in times of sadness and understanding in times of self-doubt. You know who you are.

Thank you to BookLeaf Publishing for the opportunity, and of course, to you, the reader. Thank you for deciding to read a small part of me that I made just for us.

PREFACE

I have had trouble in the past, expressing my emotions.

I have grown easily frustrated with being unable to articulate how I feel, but writing has a funny way of giving me a voice suited to who I am.

These poems are only a sliver of the thoughts I constantly face, but it was narrative medicine, in the sense I could put my emotions into words without fear of being misunderstood.

If you can't decide what you are feeling, don't worry. Go forth and find what it means to feel, in your own way, with a little piece of someone else placed in your hands, through words on paper, bound by a cover.

craving

I am an escapist on the edge of the world.
Teetering on the points of my toes,
Traipsing the fine line of reality.
In my calloused hands lay my splintered heart.
I balance the beating organ,
Yet it bleeds in sketpic fragments.
It yearns to leap from the wire I skillfully walk
upon,
To carve its own path.
Its muddled flesh has no words,
Yet I read it like scripture.
I know exactly where it wants to be,
And it is aching to be full.
Find out why, and then,
Find a sweet disposition in wanting to know
why.

dubiety

2

I am the sun, wishing to be the moon.
So that I may bear witness,
To circumambient stars.
I've failed to remember who I am.

admittance

3

I am a hypocrite.
For sometimes I am unable,
To let my temper fade.
For sometimes the betrayal,
Has rotted my insides.
For sometimes I cannot,
Let things go.
No matter how much,
I say I will.
The frustration is overwhelming,
I want to be free of the worry,
That plagues me.
It is a work in progress.

nostalgia

In Greek, meaning pain from an old wound.
It has universally become, simply and not so simply,
Longing much stronger than a mere memory.
If we could bottle the tenderness of this feeling,
We would fill until our cups were full.
Becoming a swirling, enigmatic nectar of the past.
Only for us to spill into the present,
Watching it bleed into the future.
We ache to go back,
To the point where the root of desire,
Has embedded itself so deeply into our souls.
A moment, a taste, a touch, a scent,
Will transport us back for a fleeting moment.
Clasp these moments firmly,
Because what makes reminiscing so vital,
Is knowing that we will never experience,
The poignant magnitude of these feelings,
To the fullest of beauty,
Ever again.

bonded

Losing a friend,
In my definition,
Wounds oneself,
More than a heartbreak.
When staying up all night,
With laughter gushing from your core,
Paired with a palpable sense of belonging,
And the feeling of recognition,
Steadily begins to wither.
The masquerade ends when,
You realize it won't be the same again.
They've moved on, dear.
As those feelings of listliness set in,
Don't harbour dark thoughts.
Cast them into the void,
Along with your cries of anger,
Along with the hollow cloud of fear.
The fragment they took out of you,
Will fill a cavity in their soul.
Learn to trust again, because its time,
To make room for others,
Who want to see you grow.
So plant the jovial memories in your mind,
Nurture them for time to come.
They may have been passing characters,

But your story has long to go.
Dog-ear the chapters you wish to return to,
And keep flipping the pages.

dread

The fruit flies seek the saccharine flesh of my
brain,
They want the syrup from my sweetest
memories.
Leave the pit in the middle, it sits like a stone.
The weight is a reminder.
Surrounded and buried within the fruit,
Within the flesh.
Oh, but they're in my ears,
I listen to their voices.
And they're in my eyes,
They're all I see.
The withering bodies, fluttering, stalling,
crawling,
The translucent wings carry them, in a daze.
But what they don't know won't hurt them.
They only seek the flesh.
Flies to fruit,
We all follow suit.

envy

8

I find myself confined to a cage.
The green-eyed monster paces,
In the corner, its eyes locked,
On me, its prey.
An audience comes to watch,
This dance between us.
I long to be a part of the crowd,
Hidden from the view of those,
Taunting and teasing,
Observing my discontent,
As an outlandish spectacle.
I want to be fearless,
Swallowing swords.
To taste the metallic sweetness,
Of triumph.

despondency

When I was young,
I envisioned my future self.
 In my naive mind,
 I had become something akin,
To a grandiose figure.
I carved the very same pedestal,
I placed myself upon.
I was far from quiet in my youth,
My childhood was splendid.
I was raised to work hard,
And work hard I did.
Over time, I began to create,
These expectations of who I was,
And who I ultimately had to become.
The storyteller I am, I feigned from which,
Direction these expectations unfurled.
I told myself,
"Others want me to be…"
But it was a hollow shout,
into a stained mirror.
I could not see the reflection,
My eyes peered back at me.
Rose coloured glasses a hellish hue,
Unable to accept.
My courage continuously swallowed,

By the twister.
Oh my!
I am a lion without its mane.

sonder

Sitting on a train,
Going backwards.
Accompanied by strangers,
But alone in thought.
I make quiet conversation,
With the passing scenery,
Beyond the window.
I imagine I am within a story,
Perhaps in a different part of the world,
And perhaps heading towards,
 Something incredible.
While lost in thought, I am reminded,
There are others that have lives just as I.
I accept them passing by on my journey,
And wonder if they have as rampant,
An imagination as I.

ignominy

I am a museum.
I hold treasures rarely seen.
But I allow you to appreciate my art,
Because I believe,
You understand my craft.
I offer a place for you to marvel at,
What others could only imagine.
I become a vessel for your amusement,
But when you began crossing,
The velvet ropes strung up,
You disregarded the beauty,
You've seen with your eyes.
I guilt myself into believing that,
This artwork has become yours.
Once you've taken what you wanted,
Once you've destroyed what you despised,
You flee without a second glance.
But you've left the doors open.

acrimony

Clenched fists, trembling frame.
The gnawing ache in my gut sits heavy,
 As if a dense ember weighs me down.
The fire seethes in my throat, melding hoarse
vocal cords.
Raised arms, sharp tongue, lungs in respiration,
The gnashing of teeth and forbidden words.
Can't be unsaid, they will only linger,
Suspended in the air as voiceless echoes.
A step forward, one step back, the war rages on,
Without a winner.

rue

I harbour deep culpability,
For not pursuing my ambitions.
Thinking I was not capable,
Believing that time had run out.
Subconsciously, I had upended the hour glass,
Without waiting for the game,
To officially begin.
I had bought borrowed time,
I did not need.
My passion lies there,
Deeply embedded in the sand.
For I felt it did not deserve,
To see daylight.

solace

15

There is something simple in the way autumn
leaves fall,
Like an innocent childhood secret tumbles from
an eager mouth.
Fluttering like indelicate butterflies in a
spontaneous rhythm dance,
The leaves descend without direction.
Burnt orange and auburn in colour,
They are a stark contrast against the grey skies.
Sit there and play in the mound of carnelian
husks,
Feel them crumble between your fingertips.
Know that time has been spent well,
And that the elementary way of how autumn
leaves fall,
Contradicts the byzantine mind.

relief

My fingers brushed against,
The soft and slender body,
Of a praying mantis.
Without knowing,
I had disturbed its tranquility.
The startling moment,
Suspended my movements.
I settled in the dirt,
As the mantis perched itself,
At the edge,
Of my grandfather's grave.
Now that I could see it,
Complacent on marble stone,
Stoic, unbothered, it resumed,
Cleaning itself.
Mere interactions such as these,
Remind me of the way nature,
Co-exists.
I said hello and thanked my grandfather,
If he happened to bring a friend,
For me to converse with.
Humans often forget,
What it would be to sit as still,
And as peaceful,
As a praying mantis.

tranquil

There is a place I go to in my dreams,
Let me paint you a picture.
Where grassy knolls overlook,
A mellifluous sea.
The breeze is gentle, dizzying enough,
 To softly sway the bumblebees,
 Nestled within the blueweed.
 And courteous enough,
 To carry the smell of seafoam.
Leave your busy day behind,
Drink in this moment with me.

awe

I sense that I am a mosaic,
Made from all of those I have encountered.
Stained glass, finely preserved.
Modelled by their sentiments,
Curated by their ideologies.
Sunlight cascades through,
Casting colourful beams,
Scattering them across the floor.
Uniquely individual, yet,
Uniformly human.
Someone's favourite song,
Finds itself on your playlist.
One friend's preference is tea,
So you try the taste of Earl Grey.
To tell them later on how much,
You enjoy the warmth of the citrus.
A past lover gifts you a moment,
Where they say how much they love,
An insecurity you bare.
Don't fret the feeling of unoriginality,
As we are innately influenced,
 By each other.
Which means, your affinity for,
Dancing in the summer rain,
Will be a fond remembrance of you,
As well.

fulfilled

19

There are some times;
When I think of me,
A grin chisels my lips.
Parting, a breath of air.
For it is not vanity,
But a true reflection of I.
Genuine light fills my eyes,
And this is how I've learned,
To be in love with myself.

extravaganza

The curtains close with gusto,
A thrumming silence falls over,
The crowd stood shoulder to shoulder.
But only for a moment.
Because when the chanting begins,
Calling the energy back to the stage,
You realize it is your name,
They cheer for.
Only then are you instilled with a rush,
Of one final encore.

www.ingramcontent.com/pod-product-compliance
Lightning Source LLC
LaVergne TN
LVHW050507210726

843509LV00015BA/3040